Christmas Sticker Book

Designed and illustrated by
Stella Baggott

Written by Lucy Bowman

Contents

You will find all the stickers in the middle of the book. There are also some extra stickers and labels which you can use in the book or on your own cards and gifts.

Waiting for Santa

The countdown to Christmas has begun.
Each day in December, find the sticker
that matches the date, and press it onto
the right window on these pages.

Making treats

The bears are very busy. They are working as fast as they can to make lots of gingerbread, candy canes and lollipops for Christmas. Fill the tables and shelves with stickers and give each bear a festive hat.

Penguin land

It's Christmas in Antarctica and it's freezing cold. One little penguin is alone on the ice, waiting for all his friends to arrive. Cover the ice and mountains with penguin stickers so they can play games and swap presents.

Tinsel town

Tinsel town is quiet, but soon it will be bustling with Christmas shoppers. Use the stickers to make the street look busy and decorate the windows with shiny toys, pretty gifts and tasty cakes.

Toy shop

Gifts

Building snowmen

Thick, fluffy snow has fallen in the forest and the mice are building funny snowmen. There are lots of stickers you can use to build snowmen too. Give them arms, carrots for noses, and decorate them with buttons, hats and scarves.

Singing birds

Up in the trees, the songbirds are gathering together to sing Christmas carols. The squirrels have come to listen to their friends tweeting and twittering. They may even join in the singing! Fill the branches with more singing birds and musical notes.

Decorating the tree

The red robins are hanging beads on the Christmas tree. Finish decorating the tree by adding toys, gifts and ornaments to the branches.

Santa's workshop

Christmas is drawing nearer and nearer. Santa's elves are very busy making and wrapping the presents for Santa to deliver. Use the stickers to fill Santa's workshop with lots of elves and presents.

Reindeer diets

Making Toys

How to drive a sleigh

Elves' Entrance

Magic Tools

Santa

Letters

Santa's sleigh

Santa and his magical reindeer are flying over a snowy village, pulling a sparkly sleigh. Fill up Santa's sack with presents, and decorate the landscape with tiny houses, snowflakes and trees.

Christmas morning

The baby bunnies are very excited - they can't wait to open their presents! Decorate the tree, hang stockings by the fire and give the bunnies lots of presents.

Series editor: Fiona Watt
First published in 2007 by Usborne Publishing Ltd., 83-85 Saffron Hill, London, EC1N 8RT, England www.usborne.com Copyright © 2007 Usborne Publishing Ltd.
First published in America in 2007. U.E. Printed in Malaysia.